To my favorite Niece

This book didn't turn me on at all,
But I thought that you might enjoy it.

Your favorite Uncle

In Praise of
DOLLHOUSES

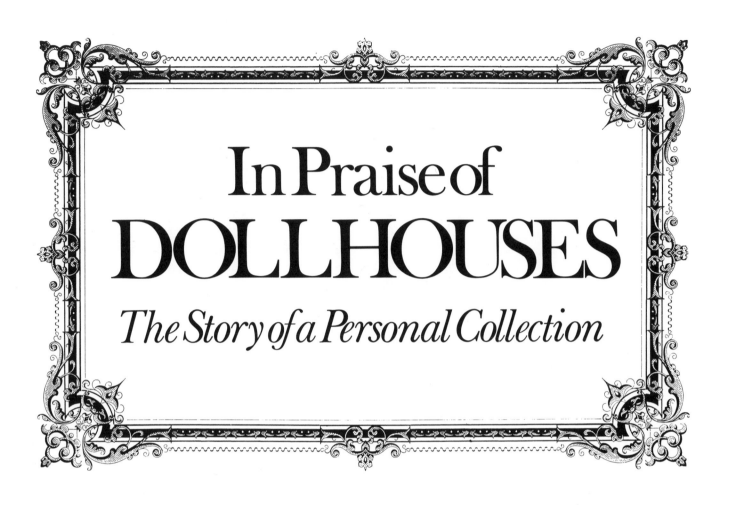

In Praise of
DOLLHOUSES
The Story of a Personal Collection

Catherine Dorris Callicott & Lawson Holderness
Photographs by Robert Brandau

WILLIAM MORROW AND COMPANY, INC.
New York

Acknowledgments

Lawson Holderness joins me in expressing our thanks to our able photographer, Robert Brandau; to his assistant for this book, Carol Akin; to Goulding Trousdale, Jr., for his assistance at the time of photographing; to our respective families and friends for their help and encouragement; and to our friend and editor, Narcisse Chamberlain.

C.D.C.

BOOK DESIGN BY SALLIE BALDWIN/ANTLER & BALDWIN, INC.

Library of Congress Cataloging in Publication Data

Callicott, Catherine Dorris.
In praise of dollhouses.

1. Doll-houses. I. Holderness, Lawson, joint author. II. Title.
TT175.3.C34   745.59′23′0740168   78-17316
ISBN 0-688-03328-8

Printed in the United States of America.

First Edition
1 2 3 4 5 6 7 8 9 10

Contents

To our daughters
Dorris Callicott Douglass
and
Rebecca Porter Holderness

The Dollhouse Room

Introduction

This collection began in my childhood when my parents gave me a large walnut open-front cabinet with three shelves to use as a dollhouse. I was allowed to paper the interior and partition it with cardboard, but not to change the exterior in any way. I spent many happy hours with my so-called dollhouse, but I did long for one that was like a real house. In the 1920s, many of the ladies' magazines carried articles on how to build a dollhouse, and I saved each one in the hope that my father would, someday, find the time to build a bona fide dollhouse for me. That day never came in my own childhood, but, in 1945, when my daughter was four years old, he agreed to build a dollhouse for her. The long-ago magazine articles were at last put to use and a large, Southern-style house based on some of those plans was built. The eleven rooms and several hallways were filled with Tynietoy, Lynnfield, and McIntyre furniture and with Dolly Dear and Grandmother Stover accessories. A large dollhouse family, named the Appletons by my daughter, moved in to enjoy the spacious house.

Three years later, I purchased an old dollhouse at a local antique shop. This rare, well-built Victorian mansion soon acquired antique furnishings appropriate to its age. It became the home of the Appleton grandparents, and my daughter was then the proud owner of two dollhouses that afforded many happy hours to her and her playmates. But the time came when her play days, too, were over, the houses gathered dust, and the doll families slept the years away.

In 1958 we moved to another home and, as there was no attic in which to store the two dollhouses, the decision was made to refurbish and freshen them up for adult pleasure. A large upstairs room was chosen to be The Dollhouse Room, and soon both houses were restored to pristine condition. With renewed interest and added space in which to expand, I started assembling the present collection. Domestic architecture and interior design have been my fundamental interests of a lifetime. I discovered that in acquiring, building, and furnishing dollhouses, those interests could have full sway in a different dimension and I could have the fun of being architect, contractor and carpenter, collector and decorator for all types and sizes of houses. Neither time nor

Dorris with her grandfather and the brand-new Appleton Family Residence

age has dimmed my enthusiasm for the world of miniature. And now the dollhouses have a new dimension—their enjoyment by four little girls and three little boys, my grandchildren.

The Dollhouse Room has become a veritable village, with doll dwellings of diverse periods and styles, complete with shops and a schoolhouse, and with plans laid for more and different houses to join them in the future. *In Praise of Dollhouses* is an open-house day, in pictures, of the "village" as it is today. The book is not intended primarily to present a collection, but rather to charm those who visit its pages and perhaps to entice some of them to acquire just *one* house of their own to enjoy. For the world of miniature does not belong to collectors only; on the contrary, it belongs to anyone at all who delights in it.

The Dollhouse Room

Callicott Main Street and grandson Clayton Callicott

In Praise of
DOLLHOUSES

The Appleton Family Residence

(Color picture, page 36)

In 1948, the Appleton family came to live in a large, Southern-style house in Middle Tennessee that had been built in 1945. That the house was a spacious dollhouse was a very good thing, as the family consists of Birdie and Charles Appleton and their six children—three sets of twins: Billy and Hubert, Nancy and Ruth, and Charles and Charlotte. There is also the maid, y√L̈ste, and the nurse. The nurse lives in.

The house was built for Dorris Callicott, age four, by her mother, Catherine Callicott, and her maternal grandfather, Mr. Duncan R. Dorris. Dorris named the members of the dollhouse family. The construction is of ¼-inch plywood put together with screws instead of nails. The basic plan of the house and its roof line were taken from a design in an article, "Buying and Furnishing a Doll House," by Alice Booth, printed in the December, 1923, issue of *House Beautiful*. The article had been saved carefully for all those years by Mrs. Callicott in the hope that the house would someday be built. The doorway was designed and columns were added to the façade to be reminiscent of The Hermitage, home of Andrew Jackson.

Height 3 ft. 2 in.
Width 6 ft. 10 in.
Depth 1 ft. 6 in.
Porch height 2 ft. 3 in.
Width 4 ft.
Depth 9½ in.

Doris's daughters,
Claudia and Rebecca Douglass, 1977

Master bedroom and dining room

15

Replica made by Ethel McIntyre
of the early-nineteenth-century
Callicott ancestral bed

The Appleton house consists of eleven rooms and four hallways. It is three stories high in the center, with a two-story wing on each side. On the ground floor are the library, the living room, the dining room, and the kitchen. The second floor has two bedrooms, the nursery, a bath, and the children's playroom. The third floor has two bedrooms for the older twins. The stairway rises to the third floor with balusters made of wooden sticks from a dollar's worth of lollipops which all the Callicotts pitched in and helped to eat up. The whole house is furnished to the last detail. The dining-room furniture is Tynietoy and the murals are Currier and Ives reproductions taken from wall calendars. The master bedroom above has a bed and a wardrobe—exact copies of antiques inherited from Mrs. Callicott's family—made by Ethel McIntyre of California. The library walls are done in natural wood; with the exception of the rolltop desk, the room is furnished with pieces in the early American style. There is a vintage typewriter. This is important, because Mr. Appleton is an author and works at home.

16

Library and nurse's bedroom above

Living room

The living room is furnished with Lynnfield and Tynietoy. In the playroom above the kitchen, Hubert and Billy can be seen enjoying the children's many toys. The kitchen table, the benches, and the cupboard are Tynietoy and the "built-in" cabinets, stove, and refrigerator were bought at F. A. O. Schwarz. There are many appliances and accessories for complete housekeeping, including open-side toaster, mixer, stand-up Hoover vacuum cleaner, broom and mop, wringer washing machine, and so on. The furniture in the older twins' room on the third floor is all Lynnfield. The nursery has Tynietoy cribs, chests, chairs, and tables for the Appleton babies.

Nearly all the accessories throughout the house are Dolly Dear and Grandmother Stover. The Appleton family are "Twinky" dolls designed by Mrs. Ethel B. Strong of Massachusetts. By 1950, all their clothes had become rather worn and a bit dirty and Dorris requested new outfits for the entire family. Mrs. Strong graciously sent them as a Christmas gift.

Playroom and kitchen

Top, girls' room. Below, nursery, bath, and back connecting hall with bookcases against the wall.

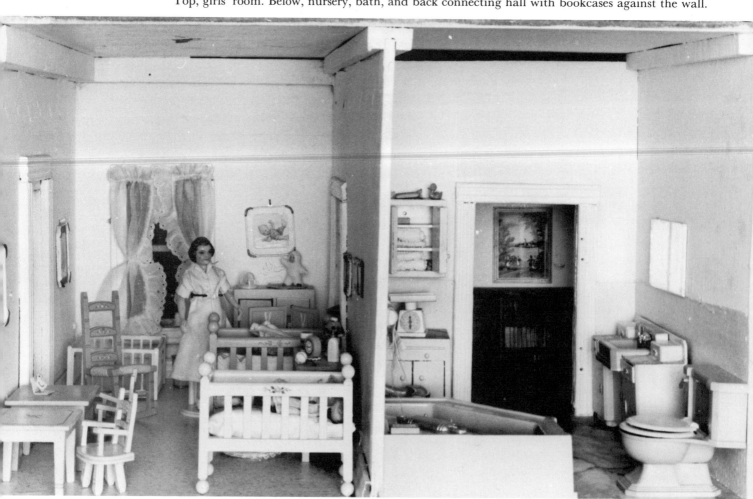

The Victorian Mansion

(Color picture, page 73)

For several months, when she drove her children to school, Mrs. Callicott passed by an "antique shop" that had in its front yard—among discarded chairs, tables, and wagon wheels—a dollhouse. Temptation eventually proved too strong, and the next thing she knew she had spent $6.50 for the Victorian Mansion. The asking price was $7.50, but her wallet held only seven dollars. It was in this house that the Appleton grandparents came to live in 1948.

The house is believed to have belonged to a child in Smyrna, Tennessee, in 1870–1875. It is original except for the lower porch and the exterior steps. The design with projecting portico is typical of houses of this period in Middle Tennessee. They often have a second-story porch, but instead this house has a bay with a very imposing belvedere above. There is a room behind the belvedere; such rooms were used for guests and at one time were known as "state bedrooms."

Height 3 ft. 8 in.
Width 3 ft. 5 in.
Depth 1 ft. 7½ in.

Porch + projecting bay
Height 3 ft. 4 in.
Width 7 in.
Depth 6¾ in.

The Appleton family, with the grandparents who used to live in this house

Open-front facade displays a
Confederate flag.

An outstanding feature of this house is the beautiful and detailed
woodwork. Both the windows and doors have moldings around them,
with boxed rosettes at the upper corners. This Greek-Revival trim is the
same as was used in many antebellum houses. The finely turned
spindles above the portieres of the two doorways in the entry hall—
which are also used for the balusters of the lovely staircase—belong to a
later period of nineteenth-century architecture. The hall is overlooked
at the back by a frosted green glass window. Upstairs, there are windows
of red glass in the side bays; the front glass is missing and has not
been replaced. The closed sides of the Mansion (not seen) are covered
with an elegant and detailed design of scalloped wood shingling.

In 1958, when it was decided to restore both the Appleton Resi-

Steps to the porch below the kitchen.

dence and the Victorian Mansion, Dorris was away for her first year at college. In her daily letters to her daughter, Mrs. Callicott described The Restoration in great detail, enclosing paint samples, fabric swatches, drawings, and so forth. Dorris saved all of these and made them into a scrapbook for her mother as a surprise present. Today it is rare documentation of changes made in dollhouses originally thought of more as toys than treasures.

Since the houses were restored one after the next in the order in which they were acquired, the Mansion was finished second, in 1960. Since that time, an ongoing effort has been made to equip it with antique furniture appropriate to its period.

At the present time the dining-room and bedroom furniture is

23

Moldings with rosettes, turned spindles, and portieres trim the doorways off the entry hall.

The finely detailed staircase is visible through the open porch.

Kitchen furnishings

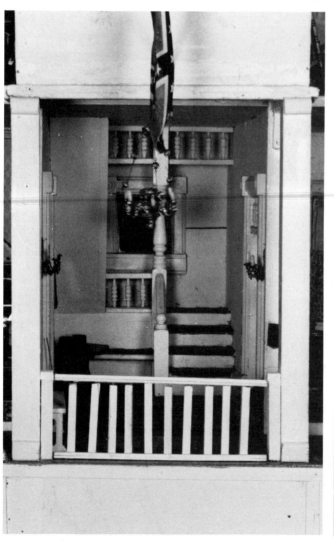

Dining room

German, possibly made by the firm Gebruder Schneegass in Thuringia. The parlor furniture, consisting of sofa, three parlor chairs, an easy chair, an ottoman, and a center table, are all original pieces made from molds owned by Stevens & Brown in 1867. This furniture was purchased in 1948—before new reproductions began to be made in 1974—so it does date from an early period. The sofa and easy chair were painted rose-color to match the rose in the parlor chairs and ottoman. A desk and a glass-fronted cabinet, referred to as "Duncan Phyfe" or "Walterhausen" complete the furnishings of the parlor.

Upstairs parlor

Today, the doll family and guests are German bisque dolls. The Appleton grandparents were provided with a more convenient contemporary house into which to retire (see page 119).

The most recent additions to the Mansion are the chandeliers in the parlor and dining room, made in 1977. The globes are white beads and the glass chimneys are made of plastic straws picked up on a trip to a local hamburger stand with the Callicott grandchildren.

The Grocery Store

After all the Appletons had moved to Tennessee, Dorris felt that they needed a grocery store to stock their kitchens. In 1950, an incomplete supermarket was bought from Sears, Roebuck. Mrs. Callicott built a case to hold the equipment and Mr. Dorris built shelves to hold the extensive choice of merchandise.

Height 1 ft. 3 in.
Width 2 ft. 1½ in.
Depth 1 ft.

Grandson Archie Douglass, 1977

The 1926 House

Height 2 ft. 4 in.
Width 3 ft.
Depth 2 ft. 2 in.

In 1963, Mrs. Callicott embarked on the project of building the first of many houses on her own. She was inspired by a visit to a friend who remembered having seen an article published in the November, 1926, *Ladies' Home Journal,* "A Colonial House for the Children's Christmas," by Edward Thatcher. It took time and many letters to obtain a copy of the magazine.

The façade is yellow, with white trim.

Front rooms

This is a double house, with rooms front and back. A few minor changes were made in the original plans: Columns, a porch, and steps were omitted from the façade; the bathroom was placed in the front; and a sun parlor with an extra bedroom above (now furnished as the master bedroom) was added at the back. At the time that this dollhouse was built, there were no ready-made parts available, so it was necessary to build the windows and doors, as well as the fireplace and the staircase.

The furniture in the dining room and in the living room is Lynnfield and includes a low upright piano. The sun-room furniture is cardboard painted to represent wicker, popular in the twenties. The occupants of this house are modern German dollhouse dolls.

29

An attractive German family lives here.

1920s kitchen. The set of jars on the cabinet counter are of blue-and-white Delft design.

Sun-room with enamel "wicker" furniture

Back rooms

Lithograph Houses

(Color pictures, opposite)

There are two original Bliss houses, *c.* 1895, in the collection. As is typical of these houses, the name is printed above the door. The paper inside is printed to show wallpaper, rugs, and features such as doors, windows, and fireplaces. The Bliss parlor set in the larger house is original (and not designed to scale). All the other furniture is German and of the period.

The three-story Lithograph House (page 33), *c.* 1905, was bought from a home in Nashville in 1954 for the princely sum of five dollars. The paper on two exterior walls is original, as is the paper on the interior of the wall that opens. This one is dark red, with three beige cats playing cards, and has the mark: "William Campbell, Wallpaper." Other walls had to be repapered or painted. The furnishings are old and there is one original chair.

In catalogues dated 1913, Converse bungalows were offered in several sizes (page 33). This house differs from the Bliss and other lithograph houses in that it is printed directly on the wood—in three colors. The interiors were printed in yellow and green and were all identical.

In 1976 Mrs. Callicott and eleven friends began to build dollhouses together. Two of those on page 33 are Bliss replicas made from Mott Workshop patterns. The third house is a school and is an original Mott design. At present Mrs. Callicott and her friends are building a church from a Mott Workshop plan.

The dimensions of the Bliss and other lithograph houses are given under BLISS HOUSES in Notes & Sources, page 137.

Lithograph Houses
(OPPOSITE)

Above, left: The Lithograph House

Above, right: An original Converse house (left)
and another lithograph house (right)

Left: Bliss-house replicas

The Grey Schoenhut Bungalow
(PAGE 54)

This house has lithograph paper on its
interior walls.

The Essex House
(PAGE 50)

Left
The English House from Bath
(PAGE 68)

The Appleton Family Residence
(PAGE 15)

Under the photographer's lights, The Appleton Residence is
clearly the historic house it was meant to be.

The Yield House

(PAGE 95)

The side entrance

Kitchen and borning room at the
back of the house

Front of the house. The roof lifts up
at both front and back.

The New England Town House
(PAGE 56)

A sturdy replica of the Tynietoy houses of the 1920s and 1930s

The Norwich House

In 1964, Mrs. Callicott despaired of ever owning that collector's prize, a fine English dollhouse—or even of visiting England. Having a husband who, like many men who love their land, travels short distances if at all, she decided that year to build her own English dollhouse at home.

Height 4 ft. 5 in.
Width 2 ft. 6 in.
Depth 1 ft. 1 in.
Stand 1 ft. 8 in.

The Norwich House was inspired by a dollhouse, built in 1720, now in the Castle Museum in Norwich, England. She based her house on the pictures and descriptions in *English Dolls' Houses of the Eighteenth and Nineteenth Centuries,* by Vivien Greene. As it was also built before the advent of miniature-lumber yards and other specialized suppliers, it was necessary to improvise in many ways. For instance, the exterior brick paper is Christmas wrapping with the glitter carefully removed with turpentine. The blue-and-white china was hand-painted by Dorris. The mantels are nineteenth-century English in design and the furnishings are also in the style of the period. At the moment, the upstairs rooms are being redecorated, so they are not quite complete in the photograph. Mrs. Callicott made most of the furniture in the eighteenth-century kitchen, which is a near-replica of the kitchen in the Castle Museum house.

In the Dollhouse Room, neighbors of the Tennessee-made Norwich House are, left, the Black-and-White Timbered House and, right, the Bath House from England.

English Dollhouse
(*c.* 1810–1850)

Mrs. Callicott's "despair" was premature, as she did acquire her first English dollhouse in 1964, the same year that she built the Norwich House. In fact, she had already had her eye on this house, which she saw at a dollhouse show, but because she is the kind of person she is, she didn't interfere when a friend wanted to buy it. At a later date, the same friend sold it to her; she was a collector of Bliss houses and this house was out of scale with her collection.

This is a box house containing four rooms. The back and sides are now the original orange-red color, as is the upper façade, which has been painted to resemble brick. The bottom half of the façade is off-white and has been lined to suggest stone blocks. To return these walls to their original state, it was necessary to remove layers of green and cream enamel paint. The only windows are on the façade, four above the door and two on either side of it. They are glass, with white outlines and lines to indicate panes. The front door is fixed and has a simple frame, front steps, and a brass medallion with a white china-head tack

Height 1 ft. 7½ in.
Width 1 ft. 8 in.
Depth 7½ in.
Height façade 1 ft. 8 in.

in the middle. A special feature of this house is the double pair of chimney pots set in the roof in the typical English fashion; they are properly placed above the fireplaces. The original chimneys, with original wood mantels and tin or other metal grates fitted in place, are built out into the rooms and rise to the roof line directly under the chimney pots.

The four rooms are parlor, dining room, bedroom, and kitchen (the latter on the righthand side, which is rare in houses of this period); they are furnished with fine Victorian miniatures. In the dining room are four round-top chairs with turned legs and upholstered seats in the style of "Dolls' Duncan Phyfe"; two more of these chairs are in the parlor with a matching sofa. The bedroom has a half-canopy bed and a dressing table stenciled in gilt with a marble top and a mirror. The kitchen has a wall cupboard, typical of this period, that may be original. Also in the kitchen is a sturdy low table with turned legs and pewter and copper accessories. Complete with lace curtains, upstairs and down, pictures, and other accessories, plus an English maid, this is a rare and charming house.

The Shore House

Lawrence Shore of Union City, Tennessee, built this house in 1933. Unlike many dollhouses, it was not designed for a child but was built for personal pleasure. It joined the collection in 1965, on loan from Mrs. Alberta Allen. The house is a double one, with rooms front and back. The exterior is covered with painted plaster to represent stucco, and the chimney is also plastered and has been lined to represent brick. The "tile" roof is made of corrugated cardboard and the floors have been scored to represent hardwood flooring. The furniture is Strombecker and the members of the doll family are "Twinky" dolls by Ethel Strong, with their hair painted black to distinguish them from the Appleton family.

Height 2 ft. 5 in.
Width 3 ft. 1 in.
Depth 2 ft.

The Memory House

Height 2 ft. 3½ in.
Width 2 ft. 4½ in.
Depth 2 ft. 8 in.

The Memory House is a bungalow of the twenties style, built in 1967 in memory of a happy childhood. The pieces in the bedroom and bath are ones Mrs. Callicott had in her childhood "cabinet" dollhouse, and other furniture is of the early twenties. The swing on the front porch was made by Alberta Allen and there is an appropriate telephone at the foot of the stairs. The family of three—mother, father, and daughter—are German bisque-head dolls of the early twenties.

The doll entrance is through the front porch.

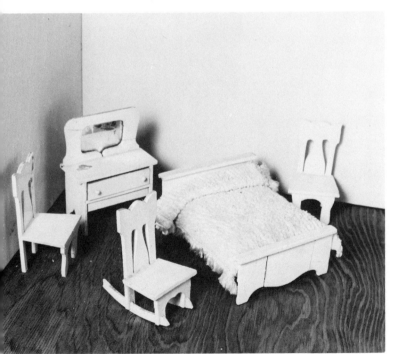

Childhood bedroom and bath sets

The Princess Patti House & The Pink House

Height 2 ft. 3 in.
Width 9 in.
Depth 1 ft. 9 in.

The Princess Patti House, below, was manufactured in 1965 by the Ideal Toy Company for the use of Petite Princess Fantasy Furniture. It is built of cardboard, has elaborate printed motifs on the interior and exterior walls, and contains the furniture intended for it. Since this glamorous and somewhat outrageous line of furniture was only manufactured for two years, the pieces are hard to come by today.

Mrs. Callicott built the big Pink House, opposite, in 1967 for the

express purpose of using the Ideal Toy Company furniture and another line made by the Louis Marx Company called The Little Hostess. The furniture is made of plastic, upholstered in satins, brocades, and flocking, with gilt decorations and "porcelain" and "brass" accessories, and was made in Japan and Hong Kong. It was designed by the two companies and the dolls, of course, were the Petite Princess Fantasy Family.

Height 2 ft. 10½ in.
Width 2 ft. 9½ in.
Depth 1 ft. 8½ in.

The Essex House

(Color picture, page 35)

Height 2 ft. 8 in.
Width 2 ft. 6 in.
Depth 2 ft. 8½ in.
There is a generous overhang

The Essex House, *c.* 1890, was purchased in Arlington, Massachusetts, in June, 1968, and restored in July of the same year. Because it wouldn't fit in the trunk of Mrs. Callicott's car, it traveled to Tennessee in the front seat and had to be moved in and out of car and motels at every stop along the way.

The house is open at the back and is furnished with antique pieces of the period. The doll family consists of German bisque dolls of the 1880s and 1890s. There is a large attic filled with the usual clutter; to get at it, one can lift off the roof altogether. Of special architectural interest are the dormer windows in the attic, both front and back; the well-proportioned chimney; details of the front doorway; and the basement windows—all visible in the color picture. To this day, real houses very like the Essex House are to be seen in many quiet American towns, which is why it is part of Callicott Main Street on page 12.

The Schoolhouse

The Appleton family and others in the Dollhouse Room community needed a schoolhouse, of course, so one was acquired in 1968 in New York State. It is a small two-room building with one room to a floor plus a front porch. It has a shingled roof and clapboard sides, and it is painted in two shades of dark green, with a little white trim. The exterior was photographed on a rainy day—as so many school days are. A simple scalloped-gingerbread trim is used at the edge of the porch roof and for the bargeboard on the overhanging eave. The schoolroom furnishings include the American flag, folding desks, chalkboards, a wall clock, a large bell, and a potbellied stove. A label on the bottom of the schoolhouse reads: "Willa Serre, Painter and Builder, Dec. 1901."

Height 1 ft. 7½ in.
Width 1 ft. 4½ in.
Depth 1 ft. 7½ in.

Late afternoon in the schoolhouse

The Schoenhut Houses

(Color picture, page 33)

The first of two Schoenhut houses was added to the Callicott collection with the purchase of this charming little yellow house in 1966. It has a red roof, a side porch with a balcony above, louvered shutters on the windows, and a front door with both pediment and pilasters. The date of the house is *c.* 1932.

In scale, Schoenhut houses were made ¾ inch to the real-life foot, rather than the usual 1 inch to the foot, and ¾-inch-to-the-foot is the scale of the grey Schoenhut Bungalow that joined the collection in 1968. Mrs. Callicott has modern German ¾-inch-scale dolls that make themselves at home in it. This Schoenhut house is of considerably earlier date—1917.

Height 1 ft. 7¾ in.
Width 1 ft. 11 in.
Depth 1 ft. 7 in. + porch 5 in.

Height 1 ft. 7¾ in.
Width 1 ft. 6 in. + porch 5 in.
Depth 1 ft. 1 in.

When these houses were advertised for sale, it was stated that they were very sturdy; the excellent condition of the Grey Bungalow confirms this claim. The exterior is painted and scored to resemble brick and stone. The roof, made of heavy cardboard, imitates green tiles, and there is a porch across the closed façade. The house opens on both sides to reveal brightly lithographed interior walls that show glimpses of fully "furnished" rooms portrayed within inoperative printed door-

Bedroom and living room

frames. This lithograph paper is all original and in perfect condition. There is a real staircase, a second floor that opens for extra space, and real lace curtains for all the real windows. The furniture is not original, but it is appropriate to the house and its 1920s style.

The Grey Bungalow is third to the left on Callicott Main Street, page 12. Its simple silhouette and comfortable front porch are familiar in small towns all over America.

Dining room and kitchen

The New England Town House

(Color picture, page 40)

Height 2 ft. 5½ in.
Width 4 ft. 2 in.
Depth 1 ft. 4 in.

This is an excellent copy of the New England town house made by Tynietoy, Inc., of Providence, Rhode Island, from 1923 to 1930. It was built by Mr. J.C. Witte of Rome, Georgia, in 1969. Mr. Witte limited the number that he would build and it was pure luck that Mrs. Callicott was able to obtain one of his strong and well-made copies. At a meeting of her daughter's doll-collecting club in Atlanta in 1968, she met a member who had ordered one but was indecisive about keeping it. Mrs. Callicott pounced on the chance to acquire it herself. It was the last house that Mr. Witte built and was delivered the following year.

Granddaughters Betsy and Emily Callicott know where everything belongs in the "Tynietoy" house (1977).

Five Peggity ladies live
in the New England Town House.

All the main rooms of the Town House are furnished with original Tynietoy pieces manufactured by the company between 1920 and 1945. Mrs. Callicott bought the Tynietoy Empire bedroom set in a dollhouse shop in London in 1972. The iron kitchen and bathroom fixtures are by Arcade. The murals in the dining room are of Old Bristol, R.I., taken from the September, 1969, issue of *Yankee* Magazine.

Three original dolls in the house are Peggitys made by Tynietoy. Mrs. Callicott's father added to the family group by hand-carving two copies of these unique jointed "people" (see page 58).

The upstairs hall has a Palladian window.

The dining room, with its
panoramic mural, and the
living room

The New Orleans House

This New Orleans French-quarter dollhouse is a Rinco house manufactured by Reid Industries, Inc., in Concord, California, in 1969. Mrs. Callicott added the gates at the front; they are made of pierced decoupage paper of Victorian design, painted black and reinforced. She enclosed the elevator shaft with copper-wire mesh and added gates framed with gilt decoupage braid. There is a pulley system to haul the

Height 3 ft. 5 in.
Width 2 ft.
Depth 1 ft. 2 in.

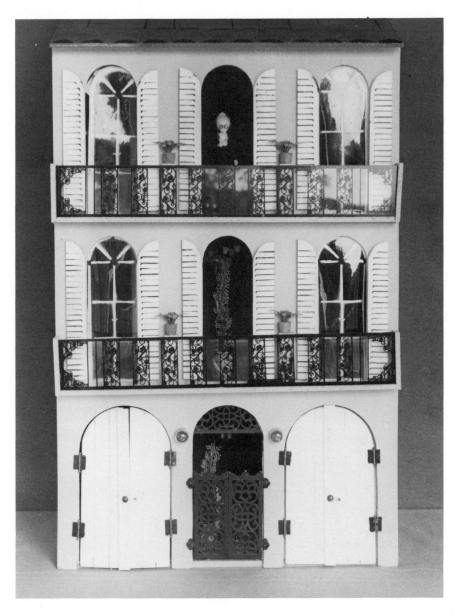

The elevator goes up when the ring at the top of the shaft is pulled down.

elevator up and down, and it usually works if a grandchild has not yanked it too hard; if that happens, Mrs. Callicott knows how to fix it.

The parlor furniture is Tynietoy, as is the yard bench in the hall below. The Victorian canopy bed upstairs is by Prescott and the rocker in the same room is by Cranford.

The mistress with pince-nez and master in smoking jacket are German dolls by Erna Meyer. The servants are "Twinky" dolls.

Upstairs parlor and study

Dining room and entrance hall with fountain

The Woodcock House

Height 3 ft.
Width 5 ft. 9 in.
Depth 1 ft. 8 in.
Ceiling height 1 ft. 3 in.

This house was built in 1934 by Mr. Clarence Woodcock of Tennessee for his daughter. It was purchased by Mrs. Callicott in April, 1970, and restored, redecorated, and furnished. A special feature of the house is the closets; they have doors and even rods for hanging clothes. The linen closet has shelves with a full supply of linens. The living room has a fireplace, with an inset hearth, flanked by tall inset niches on each side. The house has no exterior front. There are seven rooms, a central hallway, and a side porch.

Porch and living room

Children's room and master bedroom on either side of the bath

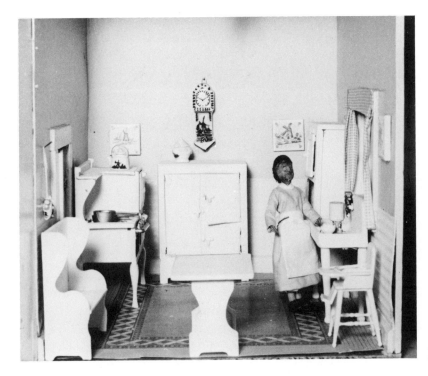

Kitchen

Dining room

The living room is furnished with Tynietoy and Strombecker and with Arlene Bellinger chairs. The dining room is also furnished with Tynietoy and has a sterling silver service. The children's room is Victorian Tynietoy. The parents' bedroom has a four-poster bed and chest by Alberta Allen and a Bellinger chair. The kitchen and bath are by Arcade.

The English House from Bath

(Color picture, page 34)

Height 3 ft. 4 in.
Width 2 ft. 8 in.
Depth 1 ft. 6 in.
Ceiling height 1 ft. 6½ in.

In 1970, Mrs. Callicott added to her collection of English houses with the acquisition of this house, which she bought sight unseen from a dealer in Illinois who had imported it from Bath, England. The house was shipped in two parts, the front arriving first and the back after a delay of several days—days of great anticipation and some anxiety.

The date of the house is between 1860 and 1870. The front windows in the bays still have the original paper designed to represent stained glass. Behind the dining room there is a small windowless room with a large side door, probably the kitchen. The furnishings are not original to the house but are of the period—mostly German Waltershausen. There are Staffordshire miniatures and an original bust of Queen Victoria from the 1887 Diamond Jubilee. The dolls are antique German bisque.

The original hobgrate

The family in the house from Bath poses with its prize bust of Queen Victoria.

The American Tudor House

This suburban American Tudor style was popular in the 1930s. The house is seen on Callicott Main Street on page 12. It was bought in a shop in Atlanta and is furnished mostly with Strombecker of the thirties period. The collie dog is bisque.

Height 2 ft. 1 in.
Width 3 ft. 3½ in.
Depth 1 ft. 7 in.

German Bisque Dolls

The collection of German bisque dolls resides in the Victorian Mansion, the Essex House, the English House from Bath, and the Memory House. They are all of the same type, with bisque heads, painted eyes, and sawdust bodies with bisque arms and legs, one inch to a foot in scale. The ladies have a variety of hairstyles, from the Edwardian upsweep with front curls to the bobbed hair of the twenties. The gentlemen are clean-shaven or have moustaches and pronounced sideburns. Some of the dolls are dressed in their original clothes, and some in copies of the kind of clothes worn during the period the doll represents. Besides the adults, there are three little girls and two boys. The one baby is all bisque, with wire-jointed arms and legs—a gift when the youngest Callicott son was born in 1948.

The Victorian Mansion
(PAGE 21)

The Betsy Ross House
<small>(PAGE 121)</small>

The bottom floor is in the cellar, below street level.

The Wythe House

(PAGE 99)

The front rooms

The Wythe House
(PAGE 99)

The back rooms

Store Façades

Left, Clock Shop; right, The Berry Book Store

Left, Dry Goods Store; center, Dollhouse Shop; right, The Christmas Shop

Clock Shop, interior
(PAGE 129)

The
Berry Book
Store, interior
(PAGE 127)

The Silver Shop
(PAGE 125)

Some of the Furnishings

Side table with punch bowl and cups in the dining room of the Appleton Family Residence

Tynietoy table, 1923, with pre-World-War-I "art nouveau" lamp, vase, and picture frame

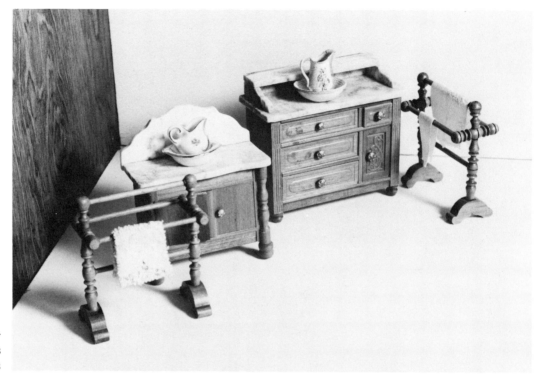

German pre-
World-War-I commodes
and towel racks

Early twentieth-century
furniture from
the Memory House

German pre-World-War-I
armoire and commodes

Period washstands:
center back, *c.* 1860,
purchased in London;
center front, designed
by Joseph Andrews, 1976

Kitchen details:
Left and below right,
in the English Black-and-
White Timbered House;
below left, in the Appleton
Family Residence

Sewing cabinets at right, pre-World-War-I; center back, Singer sewing machine
from Mexico and, in front of it, early plastic from Woolworth's, 1955

Wood and tin washstands
include pre-World-War-I at
center back, and Tynietoy, 1923,
center front; commode at left,
1902; towel rack, 1970

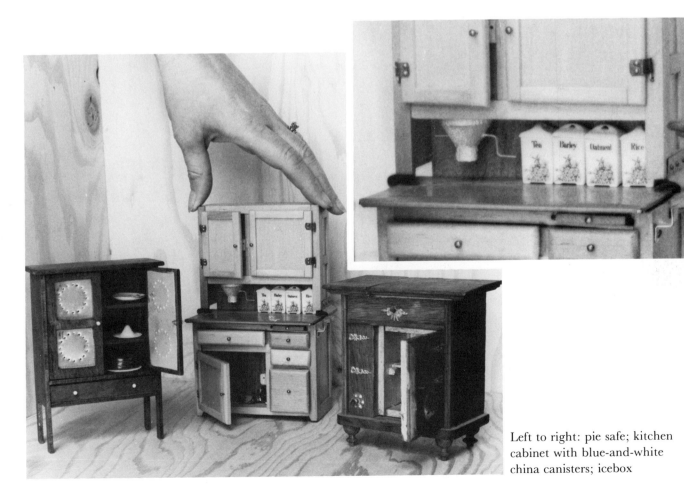

Left to right: pie safe; kitchen
cabinet with blue-and-white
china canisters; icebox

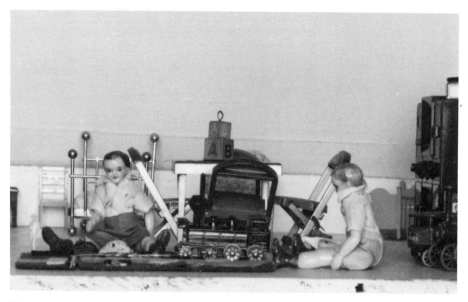

Toys in the playroom of the Appleton Family Residence

Baby buggy, *c.* 1890; child's bed, American, 1974; Tynietoy cradle

Pianos, left to right: German, *c.* 1895; German, *c.* 1900; Tynietoy Astor piano, 1923, a copy of the first piano imported to America by John Jacob Astor; center, the Appleton family's music-box piano, 1945

Rocking horse purchased in London; blackboard *c.* 1900; dollhouse doll's doll carriage, *c.* 1900

The Edinburgh House

Height 2 ft. 6 in.
Width 2 ft. 8 in.
Depth 1 ft. 4 in.

The number of English houses increased to three with the acquisition of this house in 1971, which is dated *c.* 1885. It is called the Edinburgh House because a duplicate of it is in the Museum of Childhood in Edinburgh, Scotland. However, Mrs. Callicott bought it from an Illinois dealer who had found it in Lancaster, near Manchester, England.

The windows and door are metal and there are chimney pots at either end of the roof. The house has original floor paper, mantels, and lace curtains. Otherwise, it has been restored with imported English wallpapers, brick paper, and roof paper. The furnishings are old, dating from 1880 to 1890. The inhabitants are English wax dollhouse dolls bought in Brighton.

Next page, the façade
of the Edinburgh House ▶

89

An English maid shows off two fine English kitchen stoves: Left, from the
Edinburgh House; right, from the English Tudor House.

The Edinburgh House family of wax dolls

The Edinburgh House kitchen

English Dollhouse
(*c.* 1850–1880)

In memory of Mr. Duncan R. Dorris, Mrs. Callicott's father, her doll club, "The Dixie Doll-ers," arranged for the acquisition of this charming English house. Mrs. Callicott brought it back herself from a trip to London in May, 1972, and carefully carried it onto the plane to make sure it would arrive safely. The house was impenetrably well packed, and it was a very disappointed customs man for whom Mrs. Callicott refused to undo it so that he could admire every item inside.

This is a box house, not unlike the earlier one on page 43, and very similar to the "Frogg House" owned by The Toy Cupboard Museum,

Height 1 ft. 10 in.
Width 1 ft. 8½ in.
Depth 8½ in.
Height façade 1 ft. 8 in.

South Lancaster, Massachusetts. As is typical of houses of this period, the top and sides have no windows and are painted orange-red. The facade is ornamented with projecting molding that divides the balanced front. A more elaborate molding forms a cornice at the roof line. The lower half of the house is brick and the upper floor is painted white. Both the central door and the windows are topped with wooden pediments supported by simple columns, the lower ones being curved and the upper ones straight. The fixed door has two brass rosettes.

The interior has four rooms, each with an original wooden mantel with a tin grate. All the paper is original, as is the kitchen dresser. The house is furnished with fine Victorian pieces.

The Yield House

(Color pictures, pages 38 & 39)

This early New England saltbox was built by Mrs. Callicott in 1972 from a kit purchased from Yield House, North Conway, New Hampshire.

Height 2 ft. 9 in.
Width 3 ft. 2 in.
Depth 3 ft. 2 in.

The front panels have been reversed in order to have the entrance opposite the stairs. These were moved slightly to the left. A partition was added at the sides of the stairs in both the lower and upper halls, and a closed bannister was placed at the top in the attic. At the rear, Mrs. Callicott partitioned the kitchen to include a borning room, as would

The first floor. The seam on the flooring shows the line from which improvements were made in the original plan; the stairs were moved to the left and the keeping room wall was moved to the right, to make space for a hallway. The same changes were made on the upper stories.

have been usual in a late seventeenth- or early eighteenth-century house of this kind. She also built all the mantels herself and did the paneling in the kitchen.

The furniture is of early-American design. In the master bedroom is an interesting chair. The label on the bottom of it reads: "Fac-simile

The second floor. The "Carver" chair in the master bedroom stands against the wall at the far right.

of Chair, now in Pilgrim Hall, brought over in the Mayflower by John Carver, First Governor of the Plymouth Colony. A.S. BURBANK, Plymouth, Mass.''

This is a ''museum house''; the hostess is dressed in an appropriate costume.

The attic and spare room

Part of the long slope of the saltbox roof lifts up to show the cozy paneled kitchen.

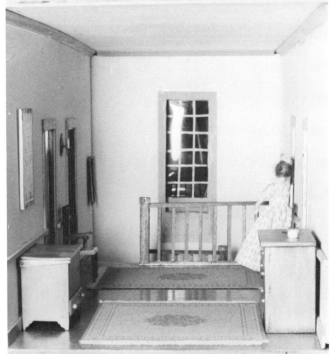

The hallways from the front

The Wythe House

(Color pictures, pages 75 & 76)

This replica of the George Wythe House in Colonial Williamsburg was built by Mrs. Callicott in 1973. The plans are from the drawings in the book *Eighteenth-Century Houses of Williamsburg*, an architectural history by Marcus Whiffen, published in 1960 by Colonial Williamsburg and Holt, Rinehart and Winston.

The large Wythe House was a fitting residence for the Honorable George Wythe, patriot, lawyer, law professor to Thomas Jefferson, and signer of the Declaration of Independence.

The outside walls and fireplace walls are made of double thicknesses of ¼-inch plywood to allow depth for the recessed windows and the fireplace openings. The exterior of the house is covered with En-

Height 3 ft. 4 in. (to chimney tops 4 ft. ½ in.)
Width 4 ft. 6 in.
Depth 3 ft.

99

One of the front bedrooms

Drawing room

glish brick paper. Interior colors, fabrics, and furniture were chosen to imitate as closely as a dollhouse can the interior of the real Wythe House. The furniture is Tynietoy and copies of eighteenth-century pieces made by present-day craftsmen.

The identical front and back of this big double house lift off entirely to reveal eight major rooms and the wide center halls. Downstairs, there are the drawing room and the dining room in front, the students' room and family parlor in back. Upstairs there are four bedrooms, two with closets. The Wythe kitchen is, of course, in a separate building—which Mrs. Callicott intends to make soon.

Opposite, the dining room

Writing chair with candle and quill pen,
desk, and table from the students' room

Students' room with law books, and one of the back bedrooms

Next page: The hallways (seen from the back),
the bedroom, and the family parlor ▶

The English Tudor House

This dollhouse of sturdy construction was made in England by a commercial firm from about 1920 to 1940. The architectural style is "mock Tudor" and the model sold for over twenty-five years. A sticker on the back reads:

TRI-ANG   Made in England   L. Bros. Ltd. London

This particular house was imported to the United States from Scotland in 1974, and Mrs. Callicott bought it from a dealer that same year.

The exterior walls are trimmed with Tudor-style wooden beams and the roof has a generous overhang. The double windows are metal, six panes to a side. A side door on the right leads from the dining room into a closed brick-floored porch with a built-in bench and two sets of windows. Above the porch, on the chimney, is a sundial "dated" 1652. Inside, the original fireplaces are missing, but early tin mantels are now used in two rooms and an English wooden mantel is installed in the upstairs parlor. The massive kitchen stove is a replacement, but similar to the ones used in early models of this house. There is a garage with a bathroom above it in the wing on the left. A sleek black Volkswagen, somewhat overscale, has made itself at home in the garage at the suggestion, it is believed, of a Callicott grandchild.

Date 1920–1940
Height 1 ft. 11 in.
Width 3 ft. 7 in.
Depth 1 ft. 5 in.

The bays of the English
Tudor House take their
furniture with them when
they are opened. There is a
charming bentwood rocker in
the bedroom. For a near view
of the massive kitchen stove,
see page 91.

The English Black-and-White Timbered House

The picket fence in the foreground belongs to a neighbor in The Dollhouse Room, the Betsy Ross House.

This house was bought in October, 1974, from the same antique dealer who had sold Mrs. Callicott the English Tudor House. A Callicott grandson was born the same day it arrived, so members of the family assumed this large delivery was in his honor—a misunderstanding that was tactfully taken care of by depositing the house in the corner of The Dollhouse Room and not referring to it again for quite a while.

This dollhouse is a fine example of timber-framed construction. Although it was imported from Scotland, it epitomizes the "black-and-white" style of homes in the Shropshire-Cheshire district of northern England. It has four large rooms, but no hall or staircase. All the fireplaces are original, as is the kitchen stove. The mantel in the dining room is quite different from the others and may be older. It is called a hobgrate and is very similar to the dining-room mantel in the Porto-bello Road Dollhouse (*c.* 1710–1720) seen in *English Dolls' Houses* by Vivien Greene.

The wallpapers in the rooms are appropriate but contemporary. We inspected them behind the fireplaces and discovered several layers underneath, the last of which could date back to more than one hundred years ago. The roof at the back can be let down into the attic, making an attic "floor" under the open dormers in the front of the roof. This is

Height 4 ft. 6 in.
Width 4 ft. 2½ in.
Depth 1 ft. 8 in.
Ceiling height lower floor 1 ft 5¾ in.
upper floor 1 ft. 6 in.
Room dimensions:
Width 1 ft. 10¾ in.
Depth 1 ft. 4½ in.

Dining room mantel

An English kitchen stove of this period is built right into the fireplace.

109

English wood-faced dolls in charming mid-nineteenth-century dress occupy the English timbered house.

The maids in the kitchen have finished preparing tea.

unusual and, if this very heavy house could be moved away from the Dollhouse Room wall, would provide an extra usable third-floor room. The furnishings are antiques of the nineteenth century, although not original to the house. There is a brass lock to hold the facade doors together, but for lack of the original key they are held closed with a latchhook. The dolls are modern English wood-headed dolls in costumes of the 1850s; they were purchased in Brighton in 1974.

Tea party in the upstairs parlor

The unusual old mantel in the dining room is at the far right.

The bedroom has formal patterned wallpaper. The clothes cupboard standing at the far left is German, of the early 1900s.

German Tin Kitchen

Height 9 in.
Width 1 ft. 2 in.
Depth 4½ in.

In Victorian times, this was a popular toy for children. It is all made of tin, painted, and has an unusual pump on the outside that sends water into the small conical sink inside. Both the oven door and the upper door in the tin stove open. There is assorted clutter of pans, pots, molds, and such, which is also of assorted scales. The date is *c.* 1856.

German Country Kitchen

This old room, *c.* 1900, is entirely original except for the stove, which is a reproduction found in a local toy shop. The cook and the little girl are modern Shaker cornhusk dolls, on loan from the kitchen on the following page.

Height 9 in.
Width 1 ft. 4½ in.
Depth 9 in.

Shaker Kitchen

Height 1 ft. 2 in.
Width 1 ft. 7½ in.
Depth 11½ in.

A visit to the Shaker Village at Pleasant Hill near Harrodsburg, Kentucky, inspired the furnishing of this room in 1975. The room itself is a sturdy, rather old apple box and the furniture is by the Hoffman Collection, New York.

The Night Before Christmas

*"But I heard him exclaim, ere he drove out
    of sight,
'Happy Christmas to all, and to all a good night.'"*

With this as the theme, this shadow box was built in 1975 by Alberta Allen and furnished by Mrs. Callicott. The dolls are by Erna Meyer, and it must be the father at the window in nightgown and stocking cap who is quoting the verse. There is a ceiling for the room, and a glass front. When it is closed, small lights can be turned on so one can see inside. The Christmas tree is by Andrews Miniatures.

*Height 1 ft. ½ in.
Width 1 ft. 3½ in.
Depth 1 ft.*

Sears, Roebuck Bedroom

Height 1 ft. ½ in.
Width 1 ft. 6½ in.
Depth 1 ft.

The room itself was built in 1972 for the purpose of housing furniture built by Alberta Allen in 1972–1973. The pieces consist of replicas of real-life furniture offered in the 1902 Sears, Roebuck catalogue. At that time, three pieces in adult size—bed, wardrobe, and nightstand—were priced at $16.95, not including shipping charges. This room is also a shadow box, with ceiling, glass front, and interior lights.

The Wilkenson-Appleton House

In 1944, Mr. Audrey Cole of Tennessee built this house for Alexine Wilkenson. When it was given to Mrs. Callicott by Alexine's mother in 1975, the front was missing, so a terrace was set up in back and some formal architectural detail was added to the back door to create a proper new façade.

Inside, a special feature of this house is that, in place of doors to the back rooms, arches are used, which allow for ready access to a kitchen and to a small back bedroom upstairs. At the time of The Restoration in 1958, the Appleton grandparents moved out of the Victorian Mansion. Mrs. Callicott's oldest granddaughter, Emily, recently pointed out that they had never been given a new home, so they are now comfortably retired here.

Height 3 ft. 6 in.
Width 3 ft. 8 in.
Depth 2 ft. ½ in.

The living room in the Wilkenson house is furnished with reproduction Victorian made from old molds of Stevens & Brown (*c.* 1867). The dining-room pieces are Tynietoy Victorian. The master bedroom has a four-poster bed by Alberta Allen. The small bedroom has a white iron bed, and the larger room in front is a well-equipped sewing room with a Singer machine, sewing and thread cabinets, and a tall mirror for seamstress's fittings. The kitchen has an unusual 1930s cabinet, stove, and refrigerator, each labeled "Henry Katz Co., New York."

120

The Betsy Ross House

(Color picture, page 74)

Height main portion 3 ft. 5 in.
Width 1 ft. 3½ in.
Depth 3 ft. 9 in.
Extension–Height 9 in.
Width 1 ft. 1 in.
Depth 1 ft.

The narrow street-side façade. There are steps leading down to a cellar room under the cellar doors.

The front rooms of the house, at the left, have stairs from cellar to third floor. There is a tin washtub and a maple washstand in the little room next to the front bedroom. The parlor has been formally furnished.

This replica of the historic house in Philadelphia was Mrs. Callicott's project to celebrate the Bicentennial. It was begun in 1976 and finished in February, 1977. It is dedicated to Charlotte Francis of Pennsylvania. With Mrs. Francis's help, copies of blueprints made for the restoration of the Betsy Ross House in Philadelphia in 1936 were obtained, and the dollhouse plans were based on these. The original building is dated 1700–1750.

Liberties had to be taken in the furnishing and arrangement of the dollhouse rooms, but the interior design and furnishings are of a typical Philadelphian residence of the early 1800s.

A larder and servants' dining hall are in the cellar.

Between the front and back of the house
are another set of stairs leading to the
second floor and to ground level and
hallways connecting the front and back.

The connecting hallways have a
removable exterior brick wall in which is
the side entrance to the house.

The back portion of the Betsy Ross House has the kitchen with corner cooking fireplace, the formal dining room above (the Flag Room in the real Betsy Ross House), and a bedroom. A head-room attic with a tiny window is above the bedroom.

The Christmas Shop *(Color picture, page 78)*
& The Silver Shop *(Color picture, page 80)*

Over the years, Mrs. Callicott has assembled a street of stores, some built from her own plans, some ready for equipment and stock. Thus it is possible for the dollhouse families to have within walking distance many of the necessities and some of the luxuries of life.

Among them is the Silver Shop, which was bought in 1975. It is well filled with only part of Mrs. Callicott's extensive collection of both antique and modern silver; there are quite a few pieces in sterling. This shop, photographed at night with the lights on inside, can be seen in color on page 80.

Meanwhile, the second shop to arrive on the scene (rather long after the supermarket of 1950 on page 27) was the Christmas Shop, installed in 1976. The shop was bought unfinished from John Noble of Atlanta, Georgia. The exterior was finished with brick paper on the chimney and shingle paper on the roof. Appropriate decorations were added and a hand-painted sign was hung above the door. Apparently the shop stays in business the year 'round, for it was open on a summer's day when it was photographed. The interior is furnished with all that is needed to decorate a house for the festive season. The attic, which opens, is used to store surplus stock.

Height 1 ft. 9 in.
Width 1 ft. 1¾ in.
Depth 11 in.

Height 10 in.
Width 1 ft. 3 in.
Depth 9 in.

English Pub

Height 1 ft.
Width 1 ft. 2 in.
Depth 8 in.

Mrs. Callicott built this room from an American Craft Patterns kit. It is really a closed case with a neatly hinged, wood-framed glass front. During visits to England she purchased the horse brasses, a "yard of ale," and bottles of port and gin. Necessary features are keys to the wine cellar, the bell to signal "time, gentlemen," furled "brollies" hung on the wall, very large tankards on the mantel, and rubber boots. A china cat has found the warmest place in the pub.

126

The Berry Book Store

(Color pictures, pages 78 & 79)

Mr. W. T. Berry, maternal great-grandfather of Mrs. Callicott, had a book store in Nashville from 1830 to 1870. The store consisted of two floors; the upper one served as a reading room, as there was no public library in the city at that time.

Height 2 ft. 4 in.
Width 1 ft. 7½ in.
Depth 11½ in.

The store is covered with brick paper; the building itself is made of two sturdy apple crates that were once used by Mrs. Callicott's father to store private papers. There is an antique iron fireplace in the second-story reading room, and all the furniture is appropriate to the period. The books were sawed one by one from 3/16-inch-by-1-inch lath and painted a variety of colors. They can be arranged to look like sets of collected works or volumes of more miscellaneous literature.

The gentleman who owns this store is a modern German dollhouse man dressed to resemble the original Mr. Berry. The store was built in September, 1977, during the time photographs were being taken to illustrate his great-granddaughter's book, *In Praise of Dollhouses*.

127

Dry Goods Store

(Color picture, page 78)

Height 1 ft. 2½ in.
Width 1 ft. 6 in.
Depth 1 ft. 4 in.

For many years, on 5th Avenue in Nashville there was a store named Thompson & Co. This store is still remembered with fondness by many residents today, so it was added to the street of Callicott dollhouse stores. The facade was purchased as an unfinished kit and Mrs. Callicott finished it during the writing of this book in the fall of 1977. The interior is completely stocked with bolts of cloth, measuring devices, thread boxes, and all that you would expect to find in a dry goods store, including a cash register.

Clock Shop

(Color pictures, pages 78 & 79)

T. Ticktock & Sons, a clock shop, was built in 1977. Like the bookstore, it is installed in one of Mr. Dorris's apple crates and is covered with brick paper. It has an extended base that serves as a storewide step. The shop is equipped with shelves, counter, and cash register and is stocked with clocks of every description, from very small ones to grandfather clocks. There is a swivel chair and a rolltop desk at which Mr. Ticktock keeps records and repairs watches.

Height 1 ft. 5½ in.
Width 1 ft. 7½ in.
Depth 11½ in.

The Dollhouse Shop

(Color picture, page 78)

Height 1 ft. 9 in.
Width 1 ft. 2¼ in.
Depth 1 ft. 3 in.

This two-story shop was also bought unfinished from John Noble of Atlanta, Georgia. Brick paper and appropriate trim were added to the exterior. The lower floor is the actual store, and it may be noted that the proprietor is a lady. This was at the insistence of Emily, who made the flat statement that dollhouses are made by grandmothers, not grandfathers. Two of the houses are miniature "Bliss" houses and a number of others certainly could be thought of as miniatures of houses in the Callicott collection. The upper floor is the workshop and is equipped with materials and tools for the building of dollhouses.

Emily's and Betsy's House

The Dollhouse Room is not a museum and the Callicott grandchildren come there to play with all the dollhouses. Nevertheless, for several years Mrs. Callicott has wanted her eldest grandchild to have her own dollhouse at home. Christmas, 1977, when Emily was nine and her sister Betsy was four, became the target date. The house was built for them during the fall of that year. It is a large, front-opening house on its own rolling platform and has nine rooms and an attic. At Emily's request, instead of stairs, the house has an elevator that goes from the hall—the room at the lower left corner—all the way up to the playroom on the fourth floor.

Next page: Emily and Betsy will be adding more furniture to their house. ▶

The *Upstairs, Downstairs* Dolls

Mrs. Callicott's method of collecting and building is somewhat chicken-and-the-egg style; sometimes the house comes first and sometimes the family. As these dolls are wood-headed dolls from England, dressed in early Edwardian style, a design of their future home must be a copy of a London town house of that period.

Also in the planning stage at present are a New York brownstone; a replica of an antebellum home in Middle Tennessee; a turreted Victorian house using the beautiful components available today; and, by Christmas, 1979, a dollhouse for granddaughters Claudia and Rebecca. She would like to build Andrew Jackson's Hermitage, but doesn't know where she would find space for it.

The Dollhouse Room: This was taken on one of the early visits, before the book was begun, which is why my pocketbook was carelessly left in the picture.

Epilogue

The Callicott Betsy Ross House was the second one I had ever heard of. The first was built by a friend with whom I did volunteer work in the New York City public schools. As we are both confirmed dollhouse addicts, a replica of a historic house seemed to us ideal to take into the schools for the children to play with and at the same time learn something about the life of early America. Ours was not an ambitious plan; rather than a large museum house—a country or city mansion— we wanted an example of the type of house that an average citizen of the eighteenth century would have lived in. And so we chose the little Betsy Ross House in Philadelphia (1752–1836). The dollhouse was started in 1975 and finished in 1976. This is the house that led, through a series of coincidences, to the discovery of the Callicott collection and the writing of this book.

Robert Brandau, our photographer, is an old friend and a native of Tennessee, as I am. One day in New York, he introduced me to a fellow Tennessean, Duncan Callicott, who told me quite casually that his mother was also in the process of building a Betsy Ross house. He suggested that I drop in to see it if I went to Middle Tennessee to visit, and that was as much as he had to say about it. I did indeed go down to spend the following Thanksgiving with good friends at their property near the Callicott farm, and I was cordially invited to see the other Betsy Ross house.

I will never forget my stunned amazement when Catherine Callicott ushered me into The Dollhouse Room and I saw not the one house I was expecting, but this imposingly large room crowded with dozens and dozens of dollhouses—so many that I could not even see where Betsy Ross's house might be. It was overwhelming and, to this day, I still feel a shock of disbelief when I go into The Dollhouse Room.

It was altogether too much to take in at once, and Mrs. Callicott kindly allowed me to come back several times. It was from her that I learned what a large community of "dollhouse people" there is in this country. As a "real dollhouse person," rather than a specialized miniaturist, she is very modest about her collection and thinks of the houses as quite special toys that can be enjoyed, on different levels, by young and old. The Dollhouse Room is a village of make-believe where the grandchildren are always welcome, a personal collection with many family associations. Located as it is in a private house, it is not open to the public and even locally many people are unaware of its existence. The lack of formal display is one of the charms of The Dollhouse Room; the collection, even as it continues to grow, remains a personal and private one.

Six months after my first visits, I was in Tennessee again for a few days and spent several hours in The Dollhouse Room. On the plane flying back to New York, I sat next to a cordial gentleman to whom I found myself breathlessly describing the Callicott collection. I was so euphoric about these dollhouses that he could scarcely get a word in edgewise, but he finally was able to inject a question.

"Why don't you write a book about it?" he said. To which I recklessly replied, "Why not?"

He introduced himself as Malcolm Magruder, sales manager for the publishing house of William Morrow. Within minutes it was established that I had the photographer we needed and Morrow had the editor. Only a few days later, it was Mrs. Callicott's turn to be amazed when I phoned to say that we had an offer from a publisher to do a book—something neither of us had ever contemplated before.

It all came true, as you have seen—an informal visit to The Dollhouse Room printed between the covers of a book. It was photographed during the hot month of September, 1977. Almost every house had to be moved for the camera. We assembled Callicott Main Street on the upstairs porch for a jacket picture. We arranged and rearranged furniture every time a house was moved—which was often! The grandchildren came to watch and to have their pictures taken, too. Eventually, we put The Dollhouse Room all together again as it had been before. It had taken six adults ten strenuous days of working with dollhouses to get them photographed and back in place, and we all had a wonderful time—which proves there surely is a special magic about them. That is why we called the book *In Praise of Dollhouses*.

—LAWSON HOLDERNESS

Notes & Sources

ALLEN, ALBERTA KITCHELL

In 1970, Mrs. Allen, the former owner of Dolly Dear Accessories, became interested in making dollhouse furniture herself. Members of her doll club soon had her working constantly to fill their orders for chairs, four-poster beds, tables, and chests. In 1972, she made the six-piece 1902 Sears, Roebuck bedroom suite, which was an instant success. All the furniture she makes is excellently designed, constructed, and finished. Mrs. Allen does not market the furniture, however, and makes it on a limited basis, usually only for friends.

ARCADE

During a ten-year period from 1925 to 1936, the Arcade Manufacturing Company in Freeport, Illinois, made metal furniture for the entire house. The designs were based on those of products sold for full-size houses at the time. Name brands were quite often seen on the dollhouse furniture—such as a Simmons bed or a Cable piano. Unlike some miniatures (such as Singer sewing machines), these were not salesmen's samples and were intended for dollhouses.

The bathroom fixtures bore the Crane label, which also contributed the design of a kitchen sink. Many of the kitchen brands are still in production today, as is Crane. The variety offered allowed the young housekeeper to have the same appliances as her mother. She could have a Hotpoint stove and a refrigerator by Frigidaire, for instance, or a gas stove by Roper. The laundry could be equally well equipped with a Thor washer and ironer and even a Hotpoint water heater.

Arcade also produced houses and cardboard backgrounds to display this furniture.

BELLINGER, ARLENE

Bellinger Memories in Miniature specializes in handmade flowers and miniature rooms. The chairs in the Callicott collection were special orders for the Woodcock House.

BLISS HOUSES

The R. Bliss Manufacturing Company was established in 1832 in Pawtucket, Rhode Island. The firm originally made wooden novelties, toy tool chests, and some lithographed toys. In 1895, it began to produce dollhouses of sturdy wood with lithographed paper exteriors and interiors. The houses came in many sizes and had elaborate gables, dormers, and porches and balconies with turned-wood pillars. There were isinglass windows and lace curtains in some of the houses, while others had lithographed windows and trimmings. As the name R. Bliss is printed on each of these houses, it is easy to distinguish a true Bliss house. In 1914 the company was taken over by Manson and Parker of Winchendon, Massachusetts, which still produces many of the Bliss specialties.

The dimensions of the lithographed houses on page 33 are:

Bliss House, large original
Height 1 ft. 10 in.
Width 1 ft. 6 in.
Depth 10 in.

Bliss House, small original
Height 1 ft. 4½ in.
Width 10 in.
Depth 7½ in.

Bliss House, Mott Workshop kit plans, full porch
Height 1 ft. 2½ in.
Width 8¼ in.
Depth 7 in.

Bliss House, Mott Workshop kit plans, small porch
Height 1 ft.
Width 8 in.
Depth 4½ in.

Schoolhouse, Mott original kit plans
Height 1 ft. 2 in. (including bell tower)
Width 6½ in.
Depth 6 in.

Converse House
Height 9 in.
Width 9 in.
Depth 9 in.

Lithographed House, large
Height 1 ft. 11¾ in., plus 3½-in base
Width 1 ft. 8 in.
Depth 1 ft. 3 in.

BLOCK HOUSE, see Lynnfield

CHARLESTON MINIATURES, see Lynnfield

CONVERSE HOUSES

Morton E. Converse began to build dollhouses and furniture in 1878 with a partner named Manson; at that time the firm was Manson and Converse. The name was changed in 1888 to Converse Toy and Woodware Company. After several other changes, it became, in 1905, Morton E. Converse & Son. At one time it was thought to be the largest firm of its kind in the world, but it is no longer in existence. The Converse house differs from the other lithographed houses in that the designs are printed directly on the wood, inside and out. The name is often printed on the edge of the living-room rug.

DOLLY DEAR

Dolly Dear, a firm that manufactured dollhouse accessories, was founded in 1928 by Mrs. A. E. Kirkland of Tennessee. The firm produced almost everything the well-equipped dollhouse needed. These accessories were designed with great creativity and were often made of ordinary objects ingeniously used to represent other, dollhouse-scale objects. They included not only such things as pots, food, dishes, typewriters, tea sets, etc., but bedding and linens as well.

In the early years, Mrs. Kirkland's son acted as her business manager. When he was drafted in 1943, a niece, Alberta Kitchell Allen, came to the rescue and ran the company until after the death of her aunt in 1948. In 1950, she and her husband, a logger by trade, continued the business until 1961. In 1958, the first catalogue was issued; prior to this time only a list had been supplied. On the cover of this catalogue was featured the house built by Lawrence Shore, a cousin, which was used to display the accessories. The house is now on loan with the Callicott collection and can be seen on page 45.

Although Mrs. Allen closed the business in 1961, she has continued her interest in miniatures and the making of them, as can be seen in several Callicott dollhouses and in the Sears, Roebuck room, page 118, and *The Night Before Christmas* room, page 117.

FEDERAL SMALLWARES, see Scale

GERMAN DOLLHOUSE FURNITURE

Germany was a major exporter of dollhouse furniture from the early nineteenth century to the advent of World War I. German furniture again appeared between the wars and some was manufactured after the Second World War, labeled "Made in Occupied Germany." Until 1891, the label of the company of origin was required on all imported items. However, the label did not have to be permanent, and as often as not a label on the packaging was all that was required. Thus it is often difficult to pinpoint the origin of German dollhouse furniture. We do know that an important center of manufacture was Waltershausen, where the firm of Gebruder Schneegass was founded in 1845. This early furniture was made in many styles and designs. The lovely "Biedermeier" of imitation rosewood with imitation ebony and gold inlay was produced by covering the wood with printed paper—which was done so well that the paper still adheres to this day.

Later furniture from Germany, dating from the late nineteenth century to World War I, often had a sturdy charm but seems to be of no special design. It was made in several finishes, such as mahogany and yellow cherry, and was also painted red, yellow, or white.

Upholstered furniture was also available, covered with velvet, silk fabric, or printed cotton. The washstands often had marble tops and there were plenty of turnings, carving, brass fixtures, glass, and what have you. No dollhouse of the period would have been complete without a parlor set of the dark-red furniture.

HOFFMAN COLLECTION

This Shaker furniture is the work of the George Hoffman family— himself, his wife Sara, and their son Mark. It is as authentic as is possible to make it, and every care is taken in the manufacturing, down to the choice of fine woods. All pieces are signed and dated by the maker.

KUPJACK, EUGENE J.

Mr. Eugene Kupjack of E. J. Kupjack and Associates is a talented and artistic miniaturist. He is well known in the miniature field and spent several years working with Mrs. James Ward Thorn on her American rooms. His work may be seen at the Art Institute of Chicago and the Illinois State Museum. In addition to model rooms, he also offers sterling silver miniatures designed after actual museum pieces. He is represented in Mrs. Callicott's collection by the Silver Shop on page 80, as well as by silver accessories in several of the houses.

LITTLE HOSTESS

In the early 1960s, the Marx Toy Company briefly manufactured ¾-inch-scale plastic dollhouse furniture. It was made in the Far East in many colors and decorated with gilt. Some of the pieces were delicate and of good design, while others were so-so. Little Hostess pieces were sold both separately and in boxed sets.

LYNNFIELD

Under several names this line of furniture has flourished for some forty years. It was started by a woodworker and cabinetmaker, Chester H. Waite, in Lynnfield, Massachusetts, in the early 1930s. At a later date, a professional furniture designer, Henry Messerschmidt, entered the business and redesigned much of the line. It was produced by Mr. Messerschmidt and his wife in their home, with some pieces made by Owen Smith, who had also worked with Mr. Waite. The furniture has stood the test of time and has maintained its quality through the years. As it has been distributed by Block House, Inc., an importer of toys and miniatures, it is often called Block House furniture.

In 1964 or 1965, with the retirement of the Messerschmidts and Mr. Smith, the company was taken over by Richard Roeder, the production was moved to Colombia, South America, and the name was changed to Andi Imports. Block House still distributes the original mahogany line and a fine walnut line is distributed by a West Coast firm. The mahogany pieces were not marked until the move to South America, but each one now has a Colombia sticker.

In the earlier line, in addition to the mahogany furniture, painted, fruitwood, and light finishes were also offered, and accessories were added in the late 1940s. Today, although the number of items offered is less, some of the original Messerschmidt designs are still available as well as several new designs.

At the present time, Mr. Roeder lives in Charleston, South Carolina, and is producing a line of miniature replicas of antique furniture of the area under the name of Charleston Miniatures.

McIntyre, Ethel

Ethel McIntyre was one of the first of the mail-order craftspeople to sell a large line of truly fine miniature furniture. She began in the early 1940s—before the advent of television, which has often been blamed for the temporary decrease in interest in dollhouses and miniatures. As the interest increased again in the late 1960s, she no longer sold retail and changed her business to wholesale; her pieces were carried by major stores and distributors.

During her years as a retailer; she had sold not only her own designs but those of other manufacturers as well. McIntyre Miniatures, which had several retail addresses in California, prided itself on workmanship and prices that were not out of line for the budget-minded. The designs, which changed little for over twenty-five years, were basically Early American. The furniture was delicately scaled and in large part handmade. Mrs. McIntyre also sold accessories of glass, copper, china, and ceramic, and bedding as well as braided and hooked rugs.

Mrs. McIntyre also did custom orders based on original designs of actual furniture which she carefully reproduced (see the Appleton Family Residence, page 16). The early furniture was marked in white on a blue sticker, "Ethel McIntyre, Alhambra, Calif." The later pieces sold through retail outlets did not always have this sticker.

Mott Publications

There are two publications issued by the Mott family in memory of Allegra Mott, whose efforts helped to found the National Association of Miniature Enthusiasts. They also maintain the largest collection of miniatures in the world at Knott's Berry Farm in Buena Park, California. An interesting aspect of the collection is that it all began with the collecting of the "prizes" in Cracker Jack boxes. The two publications are a quarterly, *Mott's Miniature Workshop News*, and *A. I. M. M. Mott Miniature Workshop News*, which comes out once a year, The first has stories on projects, diagrams, and ideas for the miniaturists. The yearly is a thick package of projects and instructions for building all sorts of things connected with dollhouses.

Peggity Dolls

Peggity dollhouse dolls were manufactured and sold by Tynietoy. They are reproductions of old wooden pegged dolls. Peggitys are 5½ inches tall, hand painted, and fully jointed. They can stand or sit and their arms and legs can be moved. All were sold fully dressed; Grandmother even had a train. There were five dolls offered: Mr. and Mrs. Peggity, Miss Peggity, Grandmother Peggity, and the maid, Nora. As they were handmade, it was not always possible to obtain a full family at one time. (It may be noted that the Peggity family in the New England Town House does not include a Mr. Peggity, although he was on order for some time.) These dolls originally sold for $1.50 for Mrs. and Miss Peggity, $1.75 for Grandmother Peggity and Nora, and the princely sum of $2.25 for Mr. Peggity.

PETITE PRINCESS FANTASY FURNITURE & PRINCESS PATTI

In 1964, the Ideal Toy Company began the manufacture of elaborate, hand-finished plastic furniture called Princess Patti. It was made in the Far East and the line included not only the furniture but also cardboard rooms and houses. The scale is ¾ inch and every imaginable accessory was made. In 1965 the furniture was renamed Petite Princess and a kitchen and bath were added. After 1965, production ceased. Thus, although Petite Princess furniture is only about thirteen years old and not in the best possible taste, the pieces are nevertheless collectors' items.

SCALE

Scale is a controversial subject among miniaturists and there are many thoughts and opinions on the subject. At the present time, the closest we have to a standard scale is 1 inch to 1 foot (1/12) and it is to this scale that most dollhouse furniture and replicas are made today. However, other sizes are available. For instance, there are miniatures to go inside miniatures; Federal Smallwares offers Micro-Mini, which includes a bed 2 inches long and a dollhouse only 1½ inches tall.

John Noble, Curator of Toys at the Museum of the City of New York and a noted authority, has graciously given permission for us to pass along some of his thoughts on scale.

Mr. Noble feels there are different kinds of collectors and that all kinds are needed. For the miniaturist who wishes to create true replicas of existing rooms or houses, accurate scale is imperative. But for the lover of dollhouses who cares most about their enjoyment and, yes, their playful aspect also, scale is not so important. Although 1 inch to 1 foot is most common, one can just as well use a scale of ½ inch to 1 foot or 2 inches to 1 foot. However, if you do intend to design a scaled replica, *all* the items must be kept in scale. This can cause special problems in finding materials that will function correctly in your design.

Scale replicas are of great importance not only for their artistic merit, but because they are useful to record the history of the decorative arts and to re-create rooms, houses, and glimpses of life-styles that no longer exist. One such dedicated miniaturist was Mrs. James Ward Thorn of Chicago, who was the guiding light behind the creation of the Thorn Rooms that are now in the permanent collections of several museums. Among these are the Art Institute of Chicago, the Phoenix Art Museum in Arizona, and the Dulin Gallery of Art in Knoxville, Tennessee. Miniaturists have done much to preserve our heritage and history.

But dollhouses are also toys and toys are meant to be played with and fantasy is an important part of play. Here we need not be so concerned with scale; the most important thought is pleasure, and what is pleasing is the most important. Early dollhouses that have survived the years clearly have not always been made with strict scale in mind—and this lack of scale in itself has great charm.

SCHOENHUT

In 1872 in Philadelphia, Mr. Albert Schoenhut founded a firm to manufacture toy pianos, dolls, and, later, circuses. In 1917, the firm's catalogue advertised "very sturdy dollhouses" that were less expensive but more durable and beautiful than imported ones. These houses were mostly bungalows. They have lavish lithographed interiors that show glimpses into adjoining rooms, wildly colored wallpapers, and such features as a lithographed "fire" in the fireplace. There is often a real staircase with nicely turned spindles. The houses open on the sides and the façades are stationary. There should be a metal label on the right side of the base that reads "Manufactured by the A. Schoenhut Company, Philadelphia, Pa."

STOVER, GRANDMOTHER

Grandmother Stover is a he. During the Second World War as during the First, European exports were cut off and dollhouse furniture and accessories again were manufactured in this country. In order to furnish the dollhouses he had built for his daughters, Mr. John Stover of Columbus, Ohio, began, in 1940, to make his own small accessories. He found that he enjoyed this and started a business that continues to this day. Stover is a very extensive collection that can supply you with all sorts of things such as vacuum cleaners, mirrors, books, *The New York Times,* pictures, irons, playing cards, magazines, and all types of kitchen and bathroom necessities.

Many firms went out of production when the interest in dollhouses waned (due, some say, to the advent of television as children's main source of entertainment). But Mr. Stover turned to party favors and thus was able to continue through the decade 1950–1960. Then the dollhouse market revived, and he has had a very extensive collection ever since.

Many of the earlier metal Stover pieces are now collectors' items, as they were made from original Cracker Jack molds manufactured by the Dowst Company in Chicago; this company is no longer in existence and as time went on the molds collapsed.

STROMBECKER

A complete line of dollhouse furniture was manufactured by the Strombecker Corporation from the late 1920s until the 1950s in Moline, Illinois. The furniture was made in both ¾-inch and 1-inch scale. The Strombecker Company was acquired by Tootsietoy in 1963 and no more furniture was manufactured. However, a new Strombeck Manufacturing Company remained in the wood business and manufactured a line of furniture in ¾-inch scale. The designs were based primarily on current real-life styles and were changed and updated to suit the fashions of the times. Most of the furniture was made of hand-rubbed walnut or cherry, some was painted. The identifying mark was stamped in gold and read "Strombecker Playthings, genuine walnut [or cherry]." Sometimes "U.S.A." was also included.

The earlier 1-inch-scale furniture was made in two qualities: Custom Built, in which the pieces were sold separately, and Delux, in which the pieces were boxed in sets. Even within the same lines, the quality varied: some of the furniture was quite good, while there were also pieces that were quite crude.

THORN ROOMS, see Scale

TIDEWATER COLLECTION, see X-Acto

"TWINKY" DOLLS

Mrs. Ethel R. Strong of Massachusetts had been interested in dolls since her teens, and this eventually resulted in the manufacture of the "Twinky" dollhouse dolls. Even at that early age, she had in mind a doll that would be different and sturdy enough to be played with and enjoyed by a child.

Mrs. Strong began her work in the miniature world by decorating dollhouse furniture manufactured by Chester Wait, the Lynnfield cabinetmaker. The Second World War brought an end to this activity, and while she was searching around for new products she received a request for dollhouse dolls, as none were available from Germany, the traditional source. Her first dolls were tiny cloth ones, but these were laborious to make and a search was made for a new material. Plastic seemed to be the answer, but it took four years to find an interested plastic maker, in January, 1964. The wife of this manufacturer was a wood carver and she made the original models. When the first of these dolls appeared, in September, 1964, the family consisted of a mother, father, boy, girl, and baby. They could stand and were jointed. They came unassembled to Mrs. Strong, who completed them by stringing, painting, and dressing them. As the sales increased, more people were needed to help, and among them were Girl Scouts, one of whom named the dolls "Twinky."

TYNIETOY

This furniture was manufactured and sold in Providence, Rhode Island, from 1920 until the Second World War. Houses were also made and sold during these years. The original designers and proprietors of the company were Marion I. Perkins and Amey Vernon. There were several styles of houses, among them a Colonial mansion and the New England Town House.

The furniture was made in many styles. An undated catalogue, *c.* 1940 or before (this date being determined from the Tynietoy address at the time), lists furniture of all kinds in styles such as Sheraton, Hepplewhite, Empire, Queen Anne and Victorian. Also listed are clocks, fireplaces and accessories, mirrors, lights, pictures, rugs, screens, and musical instruments. There were special reproductions which included several Mount Vernon pieces—George Washington's bed, a chest of drawers, a wing chair, the harpsichord given to Nellie Custis by President Washington, and a Chippendale ribbon-back chair. Also included is the "Astor piano"—a copy of the first piano imported into America by John Jacob Astor—and many small accessories such as books, boots, dishes, vases, and so on. Two types of dolls were offered—handmade, cloth wired dolls and Peggity dolls.

At one time, complete Tynietoy rooms were installed in a number of colleges and universities, including the University of Tennessee, as teaching aids for domestic science departments.

The company was sold at the beginning of World War II to two retired policemen. It is not certain when production ceased, as Tynietoy pieces were sold throughout the 1940s and there have been reports of contact with the company as late as 1951.

WALTERSHAUSEN, see German Dollhouse Furniture

X-ACTO

Long a manufacturer of fine craft tools and accessories, in 1976 X-Acto established the House of Miniatures Collectors' Series. Included in the series, besides specialized tool kits for the miniaturist, are their Tidewater Collection of furniture kits, wallpapers, needlepoint Oriental rug kits, shadow-box rooms, and "vignette" display boxes. In addition there are available individual accessories such as fireplaces, doors, windows, moldings, and furniture parts such as cabriole legs; finishing kits with tinted glue and stains as well as Modeler paints in antique colors; and solid brass hardware sold separately or with the kits.

The furniture in the kits has been carefully researched and is made to reproduce as closely as possible fine designs of the Colonial period. The parts are made of hardwoods and machined for accurate fit. The kits include a description of the original piece and its history as well as detailed instructions and the necessary hardware. If you enjoy making small things, X-Acto pieces are an excellent way to add to your collection of miniature reproductions at a reasonable price. New designs are added regularly; at present there are about thirty-five of them.